D1544244

NETWORKING
WOMEN
BUILDING SOCIAL AND
PROFESSIONAL CONNECTIONS

NETWORKING
WOMEN
BUILDING SOCIAL AND
PROFESSIONAL CONNECTIONS

LENA KOYA AND HEATHER MOORE NIVER

Rosen
YA

New York

Published in 2018 by The Rosen Publishing Group, Inc.
29 East 21st Street, New York, NY 10010

First Edition

Library of Congress Cataloging-in-Publication Data

Names: Koya, Lena, author. | Niver, Heather Moore, author.
Title: Networking : building social and professional connections / Lena Koya and Heather Moore Niver.
Description: New York : Rosen Publishing, 2018 | Series: Women in the world | Audience: Grades 7–12. | Includes bibliographical references and index.
Identifiers: LCCN 2017013813 | ISBN 9781508177241 (library bound) | ISBN 9781508178576 (paperback)
Subjects: LCSH: Business networks—Juvenile literature. | Online social networks—Juvenile literature. | Social media—Juvenile literature. | Businesswomen—Juvenile literature.
Classification: LCC HD69.S8 K69 2017 | DDC 650.1/3082—dc23
LC record available at https://lccn.loc.gov/2017013813

Manufactured in China

CONTENTS

Many people have heard the expression, "It's not what you know, it's who you know." There's a reason this has become a popular saying. While it's always important to have a certain level of knowledge about one's interests and future career path, connections can propel your future forward in a way that little else can. Developing relationships with possible mentors can provide mentees with opportunities they didn't even dream of as possible—from a spot at their dream school, to an internship that opens doors to an entire career, to a well-paying and fulfilling first job. Building relationships with experienced others can propel teens to achieve dreams they didn't even know were possible.

The process of building these professional and social connections is called networking. More simply, networking is the network of people you know you can draw on for help (and to whom you can provide help) as well as their own networks. Sometimes networking gets a bad reputation because it is viewed as being overly aggressive or pushy in order to get help from someone else. Women, in particular, often feel that they would be more harshly judged than men for networking because of gendered societal norms. However, networking provides a very real benefit in both the business world and beyond. Many studies have been conducted that show how people who network enjoy privileges in their careers such as higher-paying jobs and earlier promotions. For example, according to

Developing professional and social connections is called networking. Networking has been shown to lead to more professional and educational opportunities, and it can lead to more fulfilling relationships, too.

Cornell University's Career Center, up to 80 percent of jobs are part of the "hidden job market," meaning that they are not advertised. These jobs go to people who have connections in a company, while those who don't know anyone on the inside are out of luck. Networking is also a great way to expand one's social circle—to find the confidence to reach out to others in a mutually beneficial relationship and to even become friends.

But networking does not just need to be used to find jobs—or to find friends. It can be used in many different ways and toward different goals. Let's take the case of Zoe Hutchinson, a teen who enjoys making her own natural soaps. She has given them away to family members and friends, all of who love them and have encouraged her to sell them as a side job while she is still in high school.

Zoe decides to take their advice. But to do so, she knows that she will need to reach out to others who have started their own businesses—whether in soap-making or not—and found success. She reaches out to contacts suggested by her family members and friends and asks if she can speak with anyone who might provide her with advice. Next, Zoe creates a profile on LinkedIn. Using the connections she finds on this business-networking site, Zoe sends emails to the owners of natural soap companies and asks if they might be interested in talking with her. When someone responds to her request, she prepares a script with all of the questions she has and calls them on the phone. She takes notes as they give her helpful information about getting started. Then, she writes up a thank-you note to express her gratitude for their time.

This is just the start of Zoe's exploration into the world of small business. But networking is what provides her with the foundation to build up both her knowledge and her confidence as she moves forward. With the knowledge of so many others more experienced than her right at her fingertips, Zoe is likely to find success at her new endeavor. And for many other young networkers, developing these professional and social skills early on will allow them, too, to reach new heights in their education, careers, and beyond.

CHAPTER 1

WE ALL NEED A NETWORK

Networking might sound like something tedious that adults must do in their professional lives. It might sound like it is dull, or difficult, or even presumptuous. But networking is something we all need to do at some point in our lives. Teens might need to network to get information about a college they would like to attend, about a career they would like to pursue, or to start a club or volunteer group. Doing these things requires information from other people—it requires networking. After all, the biggest changes we make in our lives are often with the help of others.

Networking is something we all have to do during our lives, whether it is to get information about a particular college, to start a volunteer group, or to find an internship.

WHAT IS NETWORKING?

"Networking" isn't just a catchy phrase people throw around to sound important. It's actually a significant and useful tool for almost everyone. Put simply, networking is sharing between people, whether it's giving out information or services. Groups of people can exchange information and services, too.

Usually, experts describe networks as being made up of people who have something in common, such as a college major or an interest in creating a small business to sell handmade soaps, for example. But networking extends far beyond these pursuits. It encompasses organizations within the community as well as education. Maybe Devora Zack, author of *Networking for People Who Hate Networking,* defines it best: "Networking is the art of building and maintaining connections from shared positive outcomes." Networks are made up of people who want to support one another. Their common interest makes them want to see one another succeed, so they don't expect to get anything in return.

People often talk about networking in terms of finding a job, so of course networking can help teens find a first job or an internship. Networking can come in handy in other ways, too, such as when looking for a new gym, a doctor, the best pizza in town, or someone to help design a website. If someone has been diagnosed with a serious disease, networks can help that person find others who are going through the same experience, and family members can find support groups, too.

Many people think they don't have any networks and have to start from scratch, but they probably have at least a couple in place already. Each network expands with other people they know, the people those people know, and so on. Uncovering those connections reveals new people with the same goals or interests.

DIFFERENT NETWORKS

When someone moves to a new town, how does she find out where things are? An English teacher can tell her where to find the bookstore, and almost anyone local can suggest a good gym or recommend a doctor. These are examples of informal networking, and it's only a short step to formal networking, which can lead to finding a first job or getting information on college scholarships.

Family and friends know you the best and are often part of what Jeff Taylor, the founder of Monster.com and author of *Monster Careers: Networking,* calls the comfort network. This group, also called first-level connections, can be made up of neighbors,

Jeff Taylor, the founder of jobs site Monster.com, often speaks about the benefits of networking. He advises others to focus on close family and friends as they first network.

parents' friends, a friend's parents, teachers, and even service people one encounters out in the community, such as a hairdresser or a clerk at the corner store. Teachers, club members, and members of one's religious community are also within the comfort network. Obviously, it doesn't take long for the list to become long.

The professional network includes anyone in a person's line of work, area of interest, or study, such as mentors. The professional network can also be made up of students at school or college or alumni. Past coworkers, managers, and others who have worked together are also part of this group.

NETWORKING AND RISK

Networking is never a one-sided endeavor. In *Dig Your Well Before You're Thirsty: The Only Networking Book You'll Ever Need*, Harvey Mackay describes networking as working through reciprocity, interdependency, sharing, and keeping at it. He uses the acronym RISK to represent these ideas.

Networking only works when all people who are involved are giving—that is, they're engaged in a reciprocal relationship. In this way, all parties are not only helping out, but they're also receiving something in return. This may sound a lot like a good friendship, but networking reciprocity is a relationship in which

Businessman and author Harvey Mackay describes networking as the connections formed between people with shared goals and highlights the importance of reciprocity.

15

the individuals might not want to socialize with one another but are still willing to help each other out. Interdependency goes beyond people merely helping one another. The networking web is effective because all parties in the relationship benefit from it. They will go the extra mile to see that the others succeed because it also benefits them—or it's just satisfying to help someone attain a worthwhile goal. Networkers also rely on each another, such as the bookstore manager who calls the managers at other chains of the bookstore, letting them know the owner is in town. All the stores in that area get ready for the boss, and they try to look their best because one manager gave them the opportunity to shine. As people in a network become acquainted, they bond and the relationship develops into interdependency.

Networking also thrives when sharing abounds. For example, consider a local paper that is looking for summer interns. Just as it was about to post the position on LinkedIn, an editor remembered that her friend had recently mentioned a neighbor who was studying journalism in college. The editor reached out to her friend, and the neighbor came in for an interview and got the job. The newspaper was happy because it didn't have to go through the expense and trouble of posting the job, and of course the new journalism intern was thrilled to have the opportunity.

NETWORKING FOR THE LGBTQ COMMUNITY

A great way to start networking is to find a community of people not only with the same shared goals as you, but also with whom you could relate on a more personal and social level. For example, for lesbian, gay, bisexual, transgender, or queer (LGBTQ) youth, a great resource might be the Lesbian, Gay, Bisexual, and Transgender Community Center (gaycenter.org). This center offers leadership training for LGBTQ youth and networking for both college and career opportunities. They also offer individual vocational guidance, mentoring, and externships or internships. Becoming part of a larger network of people with whom you share some commonalities is a safe way to build upon your networking community—and to even make friends in the process.

While The LGBTQ Community Center is a national organization, there are many local organizations available that could provide similar services for LGBTQ youth. A quick Google search will bring up more local resources.

Finally, no network will last long if it is left alone, so Mackay tells networkers to "keep at it." Think of networking as a little like a car: a car needs fuel, oil, and regular maintenance to keep it functioning properly. Similarly, networking takes time and energy. Once it's in place, it requires additional time and even more energy to keep it thriving. Caring for a network generally means just keeping in touch with people. So even if some people aren't in contact regularly, a card or a quick note letting them know about the new internship you started or that you've been visiting possible colleges keeps the lines of communication open. It's a good habit to reach out by phone, email, or mail to someone you haven't spoken to in a while and let them know what you're up to. And always ask them about themselves. Try to do this at least once a week.

THE LAW OF 250

If the premise that everyone already has an existing network and all they need to do is tap into it seems a little far-fetched, consider the Law of 250. This rule is based on the idea that it's less about whom a person knows than whom that person's contacts know. Everyone knows 250 (or more) people, usually called first-level contacts. Each of those people also knows 250 more people. Already, that's a network expanded to 62,500 people, or second-level contacts. Each of these

Sites like Facebook and LinkedIn operate on the premise of the Law of 250. This means that everyone already has an existing network of at least 250 people that they can draw on.

19

people knows yet another 250 people, which balloons the network to more than 15,000,000. Surely someone among those fifteen million people must know about a volunteer opportunity or have information about the

It's important to do networking homework to research the person you plan on meeting or talking with. Networking homework will make your meeting or conversation that much more productive.

application process for a private high school. The Law of 250 is actually the very concept on which LinkedIn is based. Some say that with the explosive popularity of online networking today, the number 250 might even be too low.

NETWORKING HOMEWORK

Maybe doing homework is a bit tiresome, but it feels good to understand the concepts or know the facts when all is said and done. Networking homework can also have some really rewarding results. Networking homework merely involves a little research to get to know who you are meeting or the company that person works for, which might reveal what you have in common with each other. Doing some networking homework can mean making a good association great when both people have some similar tastes. Making these positive connections improves your chances for making a good impression when the new contact notices that you've taken the time to read up on his or her company or accomplishments. If you're nervous about meeting a new person, knowing a little bit about that person could put you at ease when you discover how you're alike.

Doing a little research is easier than ever before. And thanks to the far reaches of the internet, people can be gathered with a few keystrokes into a search engine. (Always remember that you should never give out your personal information to strangers on the internet. Read more about the importance of online safety in Chapter 6.) Magazines or local newspapers are also good options for learning more about local companies.

WOMEN AND NETWORKING

Recent research has shown that women and men network in very different ways. This isn't because of biological differences, but is attributable to the different ways that women and men are socialized to behave based on their gender. What

Women and men are taught from an early age to network differently. However, the way that many women network has numerous benefits in the professional world.

this means is that women are often taught from a young age to develop deeper relationships with their networks, while men are taught to build professional networks to leverage greater results. In fact, researchers Lily Fang and Sterling Huang have found that, for male and female professionals who shared the same number of professional connections, men were more likely to get more professional help than the women in the group. Oftentimes, women are fearful of being labeled "bossy" or "aggressive" by asking their network for help. This means that even if women have a large network, they might be afraid to use it.

NURTURING NETWORKING RELATIONSHIPS

Despite the fact that women are less likely to use their network for help, research also shows that women are typically better than men at forming deeper relationships within their networks. When most women network, they are apt to empower, unite, and inspire by focusing on the people around them and cultivating those relationships. They recognize that networking is about a lot more than simply making contacts. Rather than asking what a person can do for them, women tend to think about how they can support that person. When an opportunity comes up, such as a newspaper internship, women don't hesitate to recommend someone they know, like that budding journalism major.

Most women realize that business and networking success requires more than one phone call or interview because networking requires nurturing. It requires attentiveness and nourishment, even when no one needs anything. By nurturing their relationships, women can be better assured that people in their networks are keeping them in mind, too.

Part of the give-and-take of networking is sharing information. Experts say, compared to men, women are a lot more likely to ask questions and share information, which further nurtures their relationships. Furthermore, they are less likely than men to keep score about what someone did (or didn't) do.

Ideally, sharing happens because people want to help one another, not because they want to gain something from it. When someone hears about an internship opening at a publisher in a nearby city, she is eager to let an acquaintance with a background in publishing know about this fantastic opportunity. She doesn't restrict her offer to people who have done something for her recently. The best networks thrive because of the mutual desire to see people you know and respect succeed.

BREAKING THROUGH THAT GLASS CEILING

The term "glass ceiling" is used to describe the invisible barrier that blocks women and other minorities from achieving more than a certain level of success in the workplace. The term is often used to describe why women, on average, earn less than men and have fewer leadership roles in major corporations. This is not just an issue for American and Canadian women, but for women globally. According to the Center for American Progress, while American women are employed in nearly 52 percent of all professional jobs, they make up "only 14.6 percent of executive officers, 8.1 percent of top earners, and 4.6 percent of Fortune 500 CEOs." For American women of color, the statistics are even grimmer; women of color "occupy only 11.9 percent of managerial and professional positions…[and] only 3.2 percent of the board seats of Fortune 500 companies." Globally, women only earn about 77 percent of what men earn in the workforce. Although women have made great strides in the workplace, there is still much work to be done.

Marilyn Nagel, cofounder and chief mission officer for NQuotient, a company that offers

(continued on page 28)

Entrepreneur and businesswoman Marilyn Nagel believes that networking is key to breaking the glass ceiling at an individual level for professional women.

(continued from page 26)

networking support for professional women, believes that the glass ceiling can be broken in part through better networking opportunities. While family obligations and insufficient leave policies need to be improved to break through the glass ceiling, Nagel states that women can also take action on an individual level. She encourages women to take several steps, including building networking into daily work hours, identifying people who might help advance a professional goal and asking them for suggestions, and asking people in professional networks "What can I do for you?" rather than focusing entirely on the ways you can benefit.

STYLES OF NETWORKING

There may be as many different styles of networking as there are types of women. Joyce Hadley and Betsy Sheldon, in *The Smart Woman's Guide to Networking,* narrow that wide array down to three main types: matchmakers, mentors, and supporters.

MATCHMAKERS

Most matchmakers are social and delight in talking, whether with one individual or groups, as well as listening. They exude an inherent curiosity about other people, having an instinct for when to ask questions and what questions will elicit the most information. For instance, rather than simply asking, "What are you planning to study in college?" the matchmaker is more apt to ask, "What got you interested in studying journalism?" Her obvious interest keeps the conversation lively and informative.

More than just good conversationalists, matchmakers use details gathered from their rich conversations to make connections. They are the links connecting otherwise unconnected people. For example, if a matchmaker reads about a volunteer position that is open at an organization that she's supported, she calls one of her contacts there and puts him or her in touch with a likely candidate she thinks will be a good fit.

MENTORS

When most people think of mentoring, they think of the traditional definition: matching an eager worker who has a lot of potential with an experienced upper-level employee within a company. Nevertheless, mentors can be teachers, coaches, supervisors, and friends. The mentor guides and educates the young go-getter, who, in turn, can take advantage of opportunities to hone her skills. Mentors advise and coach, but also listen to the thoughts and experiences of the learner.

A mentor is an experienced and trusted person who shares her experiences and knowledge. The natural proclivity of many women to discuss deep issues and connect with others, as instinctive counselors, makes them ideal mentors. The best mentor is committed to the success of her protégé and balances when to talk with when to listen. A high school senior might approach her mentor to talk about her concerns about applying for college. The mentor can help first by listening. She can then reassure the young person by recounting how nervous she was when she applied to colleges, mistakes she made, and what she learned through her experiences.

SUPPORTERS

Women have always gathered in groups to laugh, commiserate, and give advice, helping one another in whatever ways are necessary. In groups or one-on-one, women seem to fill this support role naturally, whether they're together at a meeting or standing in line at the library.

The best supporters are sensitive as well as compassionate. They are as good at listening as they are at sharing, so it should come as no surprise that many supporters are also excellent matchmakers and mentors. They listen, advise, and offer respectful criticism whenever the situation calls for it. Clearly, this role slides seamlessly into networking as women look to their friends and connections to help them refine a clever college essay or get the word out about their new website where they are selling handmade soaps.

Nevertheless, it's important to remember that just as every person is different, every supporter, mentor, and matchmaker is unique, too. Some people are perfect to seek out when it's time to share good news about a job lead, while others might be better listeners for providing a shoulder to cry on after getting turned down by a top college. Yet another person might be good for brainstorming some new marketing ideas for your business.

THE OLD GIRLS' NETWORK

Women started to create their own small businesses in droves in the 1970s and 1980s. This effort gave networking more organization than ever before, according to Hadley and Sheldon. Many professionals argue that with this rush toward owning their own businesses, women single-handedly put the small business movement in motion.

Women worked together to connect and support one another, especially when the corporate world (known as the good ol' boy network) wasn't doing so. After years of watching the men help only one another, women around the world realized that they were going to have to help themselves. They started forming

Businesswomen like Facebook's chief operating officer
Sheryl Sandberg have taken high-profile roles in speaking about
the necessity of networking in women's professional careers.

women-only groups (sometimes called the "old girls' network") like the National Association for Female Executives (NAFE) that focus on building relationships to assist one another and sharing professional contacts. Since then, many other associations have been developed to help women network with one another and to begin to close the gap between male and female achievement in the workforce.

MYTHS AND
FACTS

There are many myths that have prevented women from participating more fully in networking communities. Here are three of the most common myths that surround women and networking, along with facts that reject these claims:

MYTH: Women aren't as good at networking as men.

FACT: Women are often socialized to be excellent networkers, although they network in different ways than men. According to researchers, women are taught from a young age to form deeper and more meaningful relationships with their networks than men. These networks can be leveraged to great success.

MYTH: Networking is only for extroverts, not for those who are more introverted or shy.

FACT: Networking is about remaining genuine to who you are. In fact, being shy or introverted can be helpful, as introverts tend to be better at listening to others, which can make others open up more and even provide better advice.

(continued on the next page)

MYTHS AND
FACTS

(continued from the previous page)

MYTH: Networking is annoying to people.

FACT: Reaching out to members of your network for help is a form of flattery. People enjoy feeling that they are a role model for others or can provide helpful insights. However, it is important to always remain polite, express gratitude, and offer to help in the future if needed for a reciprocal networking relationship.

KNOW YOUR-SELF BEFORE NETWORKING

Before reaching out to others, a new networker should know who she is and what goals she is hoping to achieve. Knowing one's own needs and desires can make that person more confident and genuine, and will help make a better impression when

It's a good idea to work on a self-evaluation first before reaching out to others for networking opportunities. This helps to get a better idea of one's expectations and goals.

meeting contacts. The best way to do this is sitting down and performing a self-evaluation before sending out that first email or dialing that first number. It's a good idea to spend some time focusing inward before focusing on others.

RULE 1: KNOW THYSELF

There's no better way to figure out how to present yourself most impressively to a prospective contact at an interview or in a college application essay than to know the answers to three relatively straightforward questions, declare Carol Christen and Richard N. Bolles, authors of *What Color Is Your Parachute? For Teens.* The questions are: What activities do you most enjoy? What environments are stimulating? And what types of people do you like to be around?

The activities someone enjoys the most and her favorite ways to spend her spare time may be excellent clues to what areas of study or career paths might be worth further

Asking yourself questions about what you most enjoy doing and the types of people you enjoy being around can help you make important decisions about your educational and professional goals.

37

exploration. For example, if someone investigating college majors enjoys art and drawing, some possible paths include studying illustration or graphic arts. If a friend's sister is in art school, she can tell you about what career paths she's considering and what classes she found valuable.

A person should know the surroundings in which she thrives. For example, a college in the heart of a big city may not be a good fit for someone who really enjoys privacy and quiet. Likewise, an outgoing, social individual may not be the ideal candidate for a volunteer position that requires a lot of solitary work, such as editing or writing.

Location is only part of the equation for determining a stimulating environment for individuals. Whether one prefers a desk or the outdoors is important, as is the atmosphere of a workplace and whether it's busy or calm or involves lots of contact with the public or other coworkers. The size of the business or school can mean the difference between a relatively small, close-knit group of people or a large, sprawling campus with nonstop opportunities to meet new people. Finally, consider the type of dress code that is expected. A private school might require a uniform, and many offices have a dress code as well. If a person knows where she'll be happiest, she has the key to where

SELF-EVALUATION FOR TEENS

In addition to the three questions provided by Carol Christen and Richard N. Bolles, teens who would like to perform their own self-assessment can answer the following questions:

1. How would you describe yourself?
2. How would your friends describe you?
3. Do you most enjoy working with others in a team or working by yourself?
4. Do you enjoy taking a leadership role or having someone else direct you?
5. What are your hobbies?
6. What are your least favorite activities?
7. Who is your role model?
8. What do you admire most about your role model?
9. What is your greatest strength?
10. What is your greatest weakness?
11. Describe your perfect day. Where are you? What are you doing?
12. Where do you hope to be in ten years?

she'll be most likely to flourish, whether as a student or a career woman.

The next step is often figuring out the types of people you enjoy being around. Many can attest to the fact that surrounding themselves with people they like and respect makes a difficult task more tolerable. The more you understand about yourself, the better you can pinpoint the sorts of people you'd like to surround yourself with at school or on the job. Christen and Bolles refer to this as the Mirror Theory. A networker should know the types of work and workplace styles where she will thrive, and she can sharpen the focus of some of her networking efforts by first connecting with the types of people she most enjoys being around. But from there she should move out of that comfort zone and begin to network with less familiar people.

YOUR STRONGEST SKILLS

A woman's strongest skills are most apt to get her closest to her goals, such as admission to her first-choice university. Talents are innate, whereas skills (also called gifts) are learned. Bolles, author of *What Color Is Your Parachute?*, describes three types of the most basic, or transferable, skills: physical, mental, and interpersonal. Physical skills use the hands and body, such as using tools or objects like jigsaws or clay. Mental skills use the brain, such as crunching numbers or working with ideas. Finally, interpersonal skills are used for helping people or working with them on their problems. Knowing several of your strongest skills can help you choose a career or area of study because you are most likely to love the jobs that require the most of these skills.

The Holland Code gets its name from John Holland, a psychologist who researched the types of people other people like to be around, which he referred to as a people-environment. His theory was that out of six main people-environments, each person has three she prefers, or her Holland Code. He described the following six types:

1. Realistic people are often assertive and competitive, and enjoy activities such as those that include nature, athletics, or tools and the five senses. They might consider jobs like personal trainer or cabinetmaker.
2. Investigative people include thinkers and observers, who are often curious and enjoy figuring things out. Possible career paths for these could include science or engineering.
3. Artistic people are creative, open, and inventive and tend to be inspired to do new things. Often they prefer an unstructured or freer environment, such as those offered in the theater, film, or writing fields.

4. Social people are thoughtful, helpful, and outgoing. They often enjoy being with others, usually to help or serve them in some way, in careers like coaching or counseling.

5. Enterprising people are talkative, persuasive, and influential. They may be good at setting up organizations or other projects as a manager or in marketing.

6. Conventional people tend to prefer rules, order, and details, which can include careers involving record keeping, data processing, and running a business.

The Holland Code aids individuals in figuring out what sorts of people they want to have around them, but it also relates to them. Most people like to be surrounded by those who have similar skills and

School counselors and psychologists can give students assessments to determine what education or career they would like to pursue based on their skills.

values, as described in the previously mentioned Mirror Theory.

ASSESSMENTS

Assessments are another option that some people like to consider. Professional counselors or psychologists can give them. Or anyone can take a test herself, which is called self-assessment. Many high schools offer written career assessments, and a guidance counselor can help go through the results.

Self-assessments can be a practical way for a person to start figuring out where her next step should take her and, in turn, who in her network can best lead her there. But such tests might seem to reduce the number of options in the field a little too much if the student doesn't remember that the assessment is only a starting point. What the test can do is highlight strengths and weaknesses, helping each student narrow down a good direction to go in a job search. The results can be a pleasant surprise, too, and broaden any search to include more options, whether it's to find an internship, choose a university, or decide what job to pursue.

READY, SET, NETWORK

Sometimes networking can happen in the moment and organically while attending a party or other function. But most of the time networking requires a bit of organization beforehand. Seek out contacts who might be able to help, and make sure to have a basic list of goals, talking points, and questions. It's a good idea to have a broad idea not only of what you hope to achieve, but also how to achieve it.

Organization is paramount throughout the process. At first, keeping track of your contacts might seem simple, but as your network grows, you'll appreciate having a system in place. Keep a record of all networking in a notebook or on a computer. Basics about each contact

46

The best place to begin networking is close to home with those who are familiar to you.

might include a name, title, and the company that the person works for, as well as his or her address, phone numbers, and email addresses. Notes about how you met, the last contact date, and a summary of that conversation will be invaluable reminders, as will the names of any referrals they provided you with, the date a thank-you note was sent for the referral or other assistance, and any other steps that you have taken to follow up. Keep all data easy to retrieve and the lines of communication open, especially the information for people such as past employers or distant friends.

NETWORKING CLOSE TO HOME

Once the organization of the network is finished, it's time to start putting the information to use. But where's the best place to start networking? Start close to home because even beginners have a network in place: the people they already know. Let's say a teen is trying to do a fund-raising walk for the National Multiple Sclerosis Society. She can begin looking for sponsors by contacting family members and friends, and then move on to neighbors, friends of parents, classmates, and graduates of her high school or college. She can probably put together a lengthy list of people to contact from among these alone, and with each call she can ask for suggestions for further contacts. From there, she can branch out into the community to members of the chamber of commerce, professors and teachers, coaches, and former employers who might support her cause. Finally, she can stretch a little further and think about professionals in the community who might be able to help, like doctors, lawyers, the owner of the health spa, and even the veterinarian. Women's organizations might be worth checking out, too, and national professional groups sometimes have chapters geared toward women.

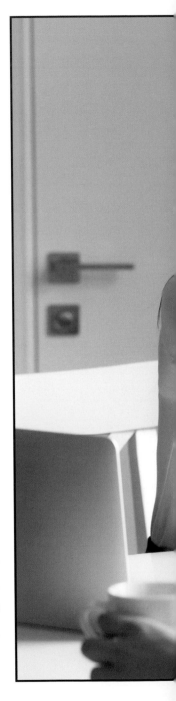

A teen looking to organize an event such as a fund-raising walk might begin by contacting family members and friends before reaching out to professionals in the community.

Beginning networkers should not feel like they're bothering those closest to them. These people know them best and are the most likely to help out. When approaching a connection for advice, keep the request plain and simple. Rather than asking for something vague like, "I am looking for an internship," the request could be more direct: "Hi, I'm studying culinary arts and am looking for an internship in the nutrition field. I thought that with your contacts, you might be able to put me in touch with someone who can help me achieve this goal." Knowing what to ask not only makes the request clear, but it also can help if nerves kick in and the would-be intern gets a little tongue-tied. Again, practicing out loud many times, in advance, is essential. To the same end, having a prepared list of questions can help ensure that all the major points are covered during the conversation. Questions keep the conversation flowing, too.

Definitely follow up after the meeting. Even writing a note to say "hello" and letting the person know how things are going is a good idea, and it's always beneficial to ask if she or he needs any assistance. This step keeps your name on the contact's mind or on the employer's radar. Always say thank-you if there is anything the person should be thanked for—even if it's just for his or her time. A phone call or an email works nicely for informal thank-yous, but a letter or note is in order if someone really went out of his or her way for you or did something big, like helped you get a job.

NETWORKING FOR SHY PEOPLE

Just because someone is shy does not mean that he or she can't network—or even become an excellent networker. However, it can seem like more of a burden for individuals who feel they aren't great at small talk or have difficulty talking to strangers without feeling their heartbeat increase and their cheeks flush.

According to Keith Ferrazzi, business coach and author of *Never Eat Alone*, shy people also tend to view networking as more manipulative or insincere than more extroverted people. It is important to remember that networking is about reciprocity and not duplicity, Ferrazzi advises, and to focus on the truth that no one can advance in their careers or otherwise completely by themselves.

Here are some additional tips for shy networkers to get started:

1. Stop apologizing when asking for help. This only shows a lack of confidence. Rather, focus on the fact that, if you are asking someone for help now, they will probably be asking you for help in the future.

(continued on the next page)

(continued from the previous page)

2. Be yourself. You don't need to become a schmoozer or an extroverted party animal. Rather, you can be genuine to yourself and make genuine connections. Being shy and humble is often seen as endearing.

3. Focus on your passions. If you are wary of going to a networking event for your college or job, focus first on a hobby or passion you have. If you enjoy books, head to a local book club. If you enjoy sports, sign up for a local team. Networking with people with whom you share a hobby makes conversation easier—and can also lead you to unexpected networking opportunities.

NETWORKING ON PAPER

In some cases, writing a letter is a more comfortable and natural way to get introduced to a potential contact, and shy people might prefer this method as an icebreaker. A networking letter is almost a pre-introduction letter, so when a follow-up call is made, the person will already be a little familiar with the individual and know how they're connected. Remember, this letter is a first impression, so it should be professional and well written. Always proofread any letters, notes, or résumés for spelling and grammar before they're sent out. The best way to do this is to slowly and carefully read out loud to yourself and get a second opinion if necessary. Have someone else you trust listen to you read the letter out loud, and have her read it, too. Another person might see mistakes that the writer missed. First impressions are important, especially for the person doing the approaching. A sloppily written letter implies a lack of respect for the other person's time and is not likely to get a good response.

Martin Yate, author of *Knock 'Em Dead Cover Letters*, gives several good recommendations for writing a networking cover letter. First, make a connection and explain how you have a mutual friend at the company where this person works or what commonalities you share. Also include a quick overview of any pertinent experience and interests. Next, explain the purpose of the letter, but never ask for a job. The purpose of the networking letter is to make a connection, and this is the point where it's more appropriate to request advice or guidance, as well as setting up a meeting or making a phone call.

Another type of letter is called a broadcast letter, says Yate. This type of letter replaces a résumé and provides a brief overview of the person's skills and talents. Broadcast letters work best if a candidate lacks a résumé or only has a little work experience. It is also suitable if she's changing careers and her past experience and background are irrelevant. The broadcast letter is also a good change of pace for a woman who is looking for a job or an internship, and she has been trying for a while and just isn't getting results. Most of the time, however, a résumé will be required somewhere along the way.

GET COMFORTABLE COLD CALLING

Cold calling is a lot like its name implies: it's contacting someone without an introduction from someone else (in other words, no prior contact) or a call for a job opening. Don't just call and hope the conversation goes well. Do some research and learn about the person. People are more receptive to a call from a stranger if there is some meaningful connection and the caller is trying to offer assistance, too.

Cold calling can be a good way to successfully network.
However, it's important to do some research first, as well as
to organize your thoughts beforehand.

Sometimes it's helpful to work up a basic script or some flashcards with notes to help keep the conversation focused, as well as some specific questions to ask. Always be polite and professional, and show respect for the person's time—don't launch into your prepared questions without asking if people have time to talk to you, and make sure you give people time to respond to you. Although it's exciting to start talking and getting to know this new person, listen and do not interrupt.

The following example offers one way to introduce yourself to a new person:

"Hi, my name is Zoe Hutchinson, and I got your contact information from your coworker Lisa Hymes. Do you have time for a five-minute conversation? [Contact says yes.] Great! Well, the reason I am calling is that I'm a senior at the local high school and I'll be attending State University next year. I'm considering a career in business and would love to set up a time to meet with you to learn more about your work. Lisa mentioned you're really active in the breast cancer awareness campaign Race for the Cure and that you're organizing a team to race next month, so I'd love to learn more about getting involved with that as well. [Pause and

let contact respond.] Do you have time to meet next Wednesday or Thursday afternoon?"

This is an example of one way to make a cold call. It can be used as a model to adapt a call that will be more comfortable to make.

WHEN NETWORKING DOESN'T WORK

Although networking can be a successful tool, it's not infallible. Sometimes your efforts aren't enough to get the opportunity for an interview for an internship or to talk with possible future professors. But don't take it to heart. In the career world, several excellent candidates may apply for a single position, and the decision of whom to choose is intensely challenging. Many well-qualified people have not even had the opportunity to interview for the job they believed would be a perfect fit. Also, it sometimes isn't possible to make a connection to attend an interview with some alumni. Of course, even if your network does connect you with some key people at a school or in a certain line of work, that's never a guarantee that you'll get the internship or be accepted at the university.

Teens shouldn't take it personally when their networking efforts don't work out. Instead, they should take it as a learning experience and improve their efforts for the next time.

Don't take it personally when things don't work out. Instead, use the experience as a learning opportunity. Review the interview, résumé, and letters, and think of ways they could have been improved. Edit the résumé and letters, and make notes for the next interview, follow-up calls, and cold calls. Don't dwell on the negative, though. It's equally important to review what went well in this experience so that you can be certain to repeat those positive points again in the future.

CHAPTER 5

DON'T STOP NOW

There's never a better time to start networking than the present moment. It can take time and patience to become tapped into a network and starting late might mean being shut out of exciting opportunities. Waiting too long can also provoke greater stress and impatience. Remember that networking should be an organic process and that people don't enjoy giving help as much if they feel pressured by a strict deadline or a stressed networker.

Not only should networking commence sooner rather than later, but it also should be an ongoing process. It isn't over when the college acceptance letter arrives or after a job

Networking isn't over when the college acceptance letter arrives or after a successful job interview. Rather, it is a continual process.

interview. If anything, networking is actually more important after that. Whether at a new school or a new job, all kinds of people will cross paths for the first time, and each individual provides the networker with a new relationship and a new connection.

Putting the network to work at a job or volunteer organization can make a person a valuable employee. Suggesting other talented employees or volunteers from your network when positions open up in the company or organization can help improve the caliber of employees, and your boss is likely to notice.

NEW JOB NETWORKING

Many first-time job seekers start with their comfort network. For example, Zoe's friends and family already know that she's reliable, a hard worker, and a creative student who likes working with natural products. By actively letting her friends and family know that she's looking for some real-world work experience, she can find out if they have any acquaintances who can connect her to another small business owner or soap maker. Often it takes time and more than a few calls and emails to get in touch with just the right person, but staying positive and persistent during the search will pay off in the long run.

It may be tempting, especially for those who are less outgoing, to apply to online jobs, send out a few résumés, and sit home waiting for offers to roll in. Picking up the phone and scheduling face-to-face meetings can help put the applicant who has gone the extra mile above those who have only written letters. Meetings are opportunities to make connections and talk up people's strengths. They can show their personalities and highlight how their expertise will benefit the organization or college.

BUSINESS CARDS

Just because a young woman isn't out in the thick of the business world yet doesn't mean it's too soon for her to think about a business card. A business card holds a lot of important information that might be useful to a new networking connection. Do you have only a few minutes in the elevator with the dean of admissions at a college? A business card is the perfect follow-up to that thirty-second elevator pitch and serves as a physical means for remembering you later on. A business card is useful for anyone starting her own business, whether it's a babysitting business or an online jewelry store. Inexpensive or even free cards can be made easily on a computer or at many office supply stores.

A business card only has a certain amount of space, so keep it simple. Start with your name, phone number or email address, and a blog or website address. Those just starting out might include their college name, type of degree, major and minor, and year of graduation. Some people like to list a few key skills or even a photograph on the back of their cards, but it might be more effective to start an account on LinkedIn and include a link to that page on the card instead. Look at the cards that people have given you as examples and see what styles seem to express you best.

Be smart and safe about the personal information displayed on a business card. A mailing address isn't necessary or safe, especially for minors, but an email address and phone number should be sufficient.

Handing out business cards is an effective networking tool, even for those who are not yet in the professional world.

If someone needs to mail something, you can share your address with that person once you've gotten to know her or him. High school students should review the information on the card with their parents or guardians and make sure that everyone is comfortable with the information that is displayed. Only give the card out to trusted connections and professionals.

It's too soon to hand off a business card after only a short introduction unless the person specifically asks for it. If a job lead or other connection is offered, however, that's a perfect opportunity to give someone a business card. It's fine to ask for someone's card after a lengthy conversation, you seem to have a lot in common, and he or she might be a good connection now or in the future. Consider offering to send the person a helpful magazine article or write an email providing a link to a handy website that the new contact might like. Often the individual will ask for a card in return, thus establishing a networking connection.

Try to keep the cards in a handy spot where they will stay neat, such as in a small case in a pocket or wallet. Keep a good supply on hand, too, because no one wants to meet a valuable contact and come up empty handed when the person asks for contact information.

THE THREE PS

According to Lara Zielin, author of *Make Things Happen: The Key to Networking for Teens*, teens can control their stress levels while networking if they use a strategy called the Three Ps. The Three Ps stands for prepare, practice, and pull yourself together.

First, Zielin recommends, teens should prepare themselves for the networking event or phone call. For example, write a script and practice it before making a phone call. This script can include what to say on a voicemail if the person doesn't pick up.

Next, teens should practice through role-playing with friends or family members. A family member or friend can play the role of a potential mentor when playing out the script. This not only will make sure the meeting goes more smoothly, but will increase confidence before going into any networking event.

Finally, Zielin states that teens should pull themselves together. This just means to pay attention to grooming and appearance before an in-person event or video conference. Zielin recommends dressing the way you think that other people will be dressing—whether this is more formally or casually.

(continued on the next page)

(continued from the previous page)

"[If] you're meeting with someone in a professional setting," Zielin states, "try to find out what the dress code is and see if you can come close to dressing the same (or even one step above)." Pulling yourself together also means attending networking events with anything you might need to maximize your experience, such as a tablet, computer, or a simple pad and pen to take notes when a mentor gives advice or gives the names and contact information of potential contacts.

AVOIDING NETWORKING NO-NOS

Although there are myriad ways that a woman can make networking work to her advantage, there are a few things that professionals warn everyone to avoid. Never ask for a job outright, although it's certainly polite to ask for advice, information, or if the connection is willing to share some contacts. Furthermore, don't be too greedy and make too many requests, because the contacts are busy, too. Always inquire about whether or not there is anything you can do to help that person, especially if it's possible to go above and beyond what the individual did to help you. Actions like these are always well received and appreciated,

Dressing professionally and paying attention to grooming ensures that you make a good impression when networking.

even when the person doesn't need any help at the moment.

Although it may be tempting to send another email when your in-box is empty or call again when you haven't received a return call, resist the urge to do so. Remember that your contacts are busy, too, and will get back in touch with you when they can. Too many calls or email messages will only be annoying or seem too aggressive and diminish their willingness to help. Busy people won't necessarily share the same priorities, so if you need to follow up or check in with someone, be polite, give the person the benefit of the doubt (don't be critical or question why he or she didn't reply earlier), and provide a very gentle reminder of who you are and why you're in touch. Most people have good intentions but can get busy or be forgetful. Don't alienate them by being demanding. On a related note, never ask them to mass-distribute your résumé or other contact information for you, and always get their permission before sharing their contact information with anyone else.

Don't neglect social graces such as having good hygiene. It might seem trivial that your skills and work potential can be affected by something like having uncombed hair, but the reality is that a sloppy appearance can be a distraction from someone's good qualities and give the impression that the applicant isn't taking the meeting seriously. Make sure that your hair, teeth, and body are clean. An outfit doesn't have to be professional or business attire for most occasions, but be sure to wear neat and unsoiled clothes and shoes. Always remember to make direct eye contact with the person in the meeting. Making little or no eye contact with the other person suggests that you are disinterested or bored with the conversation, even if you're not. Good listening can include nodding or a quick "yes" to affirm when you agree with what the person is saying. Naturally, remember to be polite, and say please and thank-you. Include a quick but firm handshake when meeting for the first time, at the beginning of a meeting, and as you leave.

10 GREAT QUESTIONS

In addition to receiving leads on potential job openings, or school or internship opportunities, a mentor can give mentees a larger-picture view of the education or career they hope to pursue. The following are questions teens can ask their mentors to learn more about an educational path or career they are interested in:

1. How do you spend most of your time?

2. What was your major in college and how did it prepare you for your career?

3. What other types of training did you pursue?

4. How and why did you choose this particular educational/career path?

5. What advice would you give a student like me who is looking to follow a similar path?

6. Based on what you know now, is there anything you would change or do differently in your studies or career?

7. What are you most proud of?

8. What professional organizations are you involved with?

9. Who else would you recommend I speak with?

10. If I have additional questions, can I follow up with you?

SOCIAL MEDIA AND ONLINE NETWORKING

Most networking today begins online or through social media. With so much information available online, it's an invaluable resource to help jump-start the networking process. This can be done in many ways. It's a good idea to create a serious social media presence online, which can include starting a blog or website. Many people also choose to put their résumés and information on networking sites like LinkedIn. Believe it or not, Facebook and Twitter can also be an incredibly valuable way to reach out to possible mentors or connections or to advertise your skills. It's important to remember,

Social media can be a great way to network online, although it's also a good idea to bring networking into the real world at some point.

however, that while online networking is an important tool, it's also a good idea to bring your networking from the virtual world into the real world at some point.

SOCIAL (MEDIA) NETWORKS

Social networks can be used to meet and connect with other people on a number of levels, whether they are personal or professional. Sites like Facebook and Google+ may be inherently designed for social interactions between friends and families, but most people have a solid core network among those very people. Users can follow businesses and organizations, and even ask questions or request advice by posting on their pages. Facebook allows businesses and organizations to create their own pages, promote themselves with status updates for new products, create events such as clearance sales, and link to other similar people and businesses through their page.

Twitter, if used wisely, can be another handy tool in one's networking toolbox, but young people must be careful about whom they connect with. Twitter enables users to follow people with similar interests, and the more people one follows, the more people reciprocate. Nevertheless, don't follow just anyone on Twitter or any social network. Try to follow people who post interesting or useful information or links. It's easy to promote other tweeters or businesses by including their name in a tweet or posting an RT (retweet) of someone's comment or link to a good article about tips for preparing a college entrance essay. People can create an account for an independent business and tweet about news, products, and events on Twitter, too.

Creating hashtags, such as #HandSpunYarnSales or #GlutenFree, can be another way to meet others with interests in selling hand-spun yarn or living gluten-free. Never give personal information to people you don't know. When used wisely, social networking sites can be effective tools for expanding and enhancing any network.

NETIQUETTE

In the virtual world of the internet—just like in the "real" world—there are guidelines people should follow in regard to etiquette. Etiquette means not only following a set of rules for reasons of politeness, but also to give a good impression to others.

It's a good idea to think about netiquette as protecting an internet user's relationship with herself and with others online. First of all, it is important to be mindful of what is shared online. Remember that anything that is shared on social media is not really private and can be seen by thousands—if not millions—of potential viewers. Also, it is very difficult to delete images or social media posts from the internet for good. These can be saved and shared by other users and websites can—and do—create caches, or histories, of information after it has been deleted. We are living in a time of unprecedented internet usage and many experts believe that we still don't know how the things we post online today will affect us twenty or thirty years from now.

Before sharing anything on social media, a user should ask herself whether or not she would like a parent, teacher, or potential employer to see it. If the

(continued on the next page)

(continued from the previous page)

answer is no, then it might not be good information to share online. This includes both photos and information that could be considered too personal or too revealing. It is also important for internet users to consider their language use online and how they communicate with others. Unlike oral communication, written communication online can be saved and referred to later. This means that it is never a good idea to say something in the heat of the moment online; you might regret it later.

LINKEDIN

LinkedIn is one of the social media sites specifically geared toward businesses, describing itself as "the world's largest professional network." LinkedIn reports that professionals are signing up to join the site at a rate faster than two people per second. And as of the close of 2016, LinkedIn boasted more than 467 million members in more than 200 countries and territories.

LinkedIn, like its more socially oriented counterparts, is free and easy to set up. It offers space to post a résumé, list work experience and education, and describe one's goals. Starting online networking

LinkedIn is an important networking site that is specifically geared toward making business connections and can be a useful tool for new networkers.

is as easy as searching a contact list, which LinkedIn can do with the click of a button, sending invites to selected people asking if they'd like to join the user's network. Users should scan through the list and choose reliable people because the connections on a LinkedIn profile can be viewed by others and are often viewed as a reflection of the users. As one's profile expands on the site, LinkedIn automatically generates suggestions for new people a user might know based on people and companies to which he or she is already linked. Users can use the site to search businesses, organizations, and people in different departments to see if anyone they know is connected to someone who is working there. LinkedIn also has a job search option.

Finally, one unique feature LinkedIn offers is a recommendations section where users can write a general recommendation for people within their LinkedIn network and vice versa. Recommendations are a wonderful networking tool that everyone can use to show their appreciation for one another.

Privacy can be an issue on any one of these sites, so be sure to go over security settings information to see how much information is being shared and with whom. Most sites allow a user to keep posts and other personal information private to all but friends or people who have been specified. You can set any of these sites to be visible to friends only, which is always wise, especially for young teens. But still, never forget that even the most locked-down personal profile is at risk, so be smart about what you're putting online.

TOASTMASTERS FOR TEENS

Toastmasters (www.toastmasters.org) is an international organization dedicated to developing its members' public speaking skills and leadership abilities. It boasts more than 345,000 members in 15,900 clubs across 142 countries. Members of Toastmasters are scheduled to give speeches in front of their clubs on various topics. Then, members give feedback about the speech in a collaborative and supportive atmosphere. Not only does this help members develop their comfort speaking in front of groups of people, which aids with networking, but it is also a great networking community itself.

For teens, Toastmasters offers a Youth Leadership Program. Teens who are already members of a Toastmasters Club can create a program for other local teens. According to Toastmasters, these two-month-long programs focus on teaching teens to "overcome nervousness when speaking before an audience, organize and present ideas logically and convincingly, listen carefully to others' ideas, and offer advice to help others improve their speaking and leadership skills." In addition, Toastmasters offers Gavel Clubs, which are membership-based Toastmaster groups specifically for teens.

CREATING AN ONLINE PRESENCE

All these sites are excellent tools, but sometimes the constraints of the site prevent someone from being as creative as he or she wishes. Fortunately, there are numerous ways to create an online presence that will enhance one's networking efforts. Many sites have basic templates that make creating a site an easy task. Once you've set up the site, you can decide how to present

Starting a blog is a great way to create an online presence while also showcasing one's creativity.

your business or experience. A neat and thoughtful website offers potential networking contacts a glimpse into a person's experience and interests and serves as an example of the individual's initiative and creativity.

A blog provides an online space to write, post photographs, and share news. Blogs, such as those offered by Blogger, WordPress, or Tumblr, can include more informal discussions about a business or interests, and the blogger can choose whether or not to allow comments to the blog entries.

People starting their own businesses might blog about products or services offered by their new company. Blog readers will learn more about the proprietor and products in this way, as well as through posted photos of the products (such as handmade lotions or soaps) or services (such as dog grooming). Like other sites, blogs can link to related pages or sites, such as Twitter and LinkedIn. A blog is an opportunity for a networker's creativity and expression to shine, but remember to keep your blogging courteous and professional.

CHAPTER 7

NETWORKING FOR OTHER OPPORTUNITIES

Many people associate networking with one's professional career. However, networking can be an important step in seeking out any kind of information, whether it is to find the perfect college, a volunteer opportunity, or to create a local group. Networking also has the added opportunity of opening up one's social horizons, which can mean making friends who share one's interests and passions.

NETWORKING FOR COLLEGE

Apart from finding a first job, the college search and application process might be the first major networking endeavor for many students. The

Many teens' first experience with networking is often during the college search and application process.

school guidance office is a great place for students to start looking for advice about colleges and other post–high school possibilities. Guidance counselors know all about researching and applying for higher education, and they can help direct networking efforts both within the school and in the community. Teachers are also a great source of information and networking, especially those who teach a subject that interests the student. Educators are solid resources for networking plans as well.

Networking through family and friends is a natural step, especially during the earliest stages of choosing schools and sending out applications. Family members who have gone into the same or similar areas of study are terrific sources, and they may have friends or acquaintances who could be helpful at certain schools or departments. Friends might have parents or older siblings who are alumni, are in a related career, or know someone in the industry who would be willing to offer advice about a university or major. These same people might have tips or suggestions for the admissions process, too.

A great cross-section of local businesses and interests exists within religious organizations, community centers, and volunteer groups. Attend coffee hours after the service or other social events to become acquainted with the people there. Ask those with similar interests what and where they studied. If they can't help out directly, they might suggest someone they know who would have more information.

Talking to alumni or students attending the college, or even accompanying them on a typical day, are great ways to meet people there and make some new networking connections.

WRITING A THANK–YOU EMAIL

After receiving advice or mentorship, it is important for teens to send a thank-you note to express their appreciation and gratitude. This goes a long way in making them stand out to those in their networking circles. This note can be either hand-written and sent via snail mail or, more commonly, sent as an email. Address the recipient by name and include some specifics from your meeting to show that the time they spent helping you was indeed worthwhile. Thank-you notes should also be sent within several days of having an interview, whether for a spot at a school or college or for a job or internship. It is not appropriate to send a thank-you note as a text message if you have the person's phone number.

(continued on the next page)

(continued from the previous page)

When sending an emailed thank-you note, it is important to keep the following rules of email etiquette in mind:

1. Make sure you are sending your email from an appropriate email address. Your email address should preferably just be your name and should not include any nicknames or descriptors like "hotstuff88@abc.com" or "partyanimal@abc.com."

2. Include a clear subject line, preferably with your name and your reason for emailing.

3. Begin your email with a greeting using the person's name (for example, "Dear Ms. Smith") and end with a closing (for example, "Sincerely, Zoe").

4. Make sure your email is properly punctuated. Use a spell checker and reread it several times before sending.

5. Keep your note short and clear. Avoid the following: complaining, gossiping, jokes, or sarcasm.

INTERNSHIPS AND VOLUNTEERING

Internships and volunteering are two great ways to make new networking connections in your area of interest. Volunteer opportunities and internships fill two functions: obtaining work experience and making new connections along the way. Volunteering can include jobs such as tutoring for an after-school program or helping out with maintenance at a summer camp. As the name suggests, volunteer work is generally unpaid, but the times and hours may be flexible, depending on the needs of the company or organization. Many places appreciate extra help, so students should get the word out with the people in their networks that they are looking to lend a hand, mentioning if there is a specific kind of work they are good at.

Some internships offer a modest paycheck, but they often only last one semester or year. They may also be a little more competitive, especially if the company is well known. Family and friends are a great place to start investigating a connection to a company. Students who are selected for internships can do some great networking while working at the company, too. Create a good relationship with supervisors and managers who are helpful on the job, as well as coworkers and even other interns—you never know what might come of the relationship in the future if you stay in touch.

Teens can use their networking skills to create their own businesses and to become young entrepreneurs.

Public trade shows are gatherings of people and businesses in the same line of work. Those looking to expand their networks in a particular field often find that these shows offer an opportunity to explore other businesses and meet people in a relatively casual setting. Meeting other people in the businesses that interest you can generate opportunities for volunteering, an internship, or other prospects.

STARTING YOUR OWN BUSINESS

Just because you haven't graduated from high school or college yet doesn't mean it's too soon to think about starting a business. History is brimming with success stories about young entrepreneurs who got going well before receiving a diploma. Contact family members and friends who are already in the field or related areas. As Zoe is starting an online store to sell her

At its most basic, networking is about sharing and connecting with others, which is something everyone can enjoy.

handmade soaps, for instance, she could contact the natural food stores and co-ops to see if they would be willing to stock her items.

Starting a blog or website is another way to get the word out about a new business. By including the link to the site on a business card, postcard, or advertisement, you can direct people to learn about the new business endeavor. This link is easy to include in emails and networking letters, as well as in résumés. A website is also easy to refer to during a phone call or mention during the elevator pitch. Creating a Facebook page or LinkedIn account for a business is another simple way to network. Zoe can simply say "Find me on Facebook" to someone who seems genuinely interested in her products. Don't forget about creating a personal or business account on Twitter, too, for posting information, updates, and connecting with other similar people or organizations.

Networking is often no more than a conversation away, whether it's using a social media site to communicate, perusing the high school alumni list for college or business connections, or simply talking with friends and family about personal matters. Introverts and extroverts alike can network—it's merely a matter of experimenting to figure out which methods work best for you. After all, at its most basic level, networking is about sharing, and everyone can do that.

ALUMNI People who have attended or graduated from a certain high school, university, or college; also former members of a club, workplace, or organization.

ANECDOTE A short, amusing, or entertaining story or narrative.

ASSESSMENTS Evaluations given by professional psychologists or teachers of the abilities or qualities of someone.

BENEFITS Services or rights, such as health insurance or vacation time, offered by an employer in addition to wages or a salary.

BROADCAST LETTER A networking letter that can be sent to a group of potential employers or contacts.

CACHES A collection of items that is stored; in computing, information that is stored online.

CHIEF EXECUTIVE OFFICER (CEO) Someone who generally makes major decisions in a business or other organization.

COLD CALLING Making a call to someone who is unknown to the caller, usually for the purposes of networking or selling.

ELEVATOR PITCH A short and clear sales pitch.

ENTREPRENEUR The sole owner of a business who is responsible for all the organizing and managing.

A person who tends to be outgoing. Groups of social characteristics and norms typically associated with males or females. An invisible barrier with a company that prevents women and other minorities from achieving high-level jobs. A group of male, usually elite, businessmen who tend to be loyal to one another to the exclusion of others, especially women and minorities. A term preceded by the # symbol used on social networking sites like Twitter to create groups of posts on that site. Existing in someone from birth; a characteristic that is seen as essential or permanent. A supervised on-the-job experience for a student. A person who tends to be reserved or shy. An acronym for lesbian, gay, bisexual, transgender, and queer; used to designate a group of people who share similar social or political concerns over sexual or gender identity.

MENTOR A trusted guide, coach, or counselor.
PROCLIVITY A tendency or predisposition toward doing a particular thing.
PROPRIETOR The sole owner of a business.
PROTÉGÉ A person who is guided or trained by someone with more experience.
RECIPROCITY The process of exchanging things for the mutual benefit of both parties.
RÉSUMÉ A summary of someone's educational and career experience, which is used to get a job, internship, or other opportunity.
SOCIALIZED To have taught someone to behave in a way according to societal norms.
TRADE SHOW A gathering or convention of professionals in a certain line of work or industry to display new products and develop networks.

American Association of University Women
   (AAUW)
   1310 L Street NW, Suite 1000
   Washington, DC 20005
   (202) 785-7700
   Email: connect@aauw.org
   Website: www.aauw.org
   Facebook: @AAUW.national
   Twitter: @AAUW
   The AAUW, formed in 1881, advances equity for
   women and girls through advocacy, education,
   philanthropy, and research. The organization
   has many different branches across the
   United States.

American Business Women's Association
   (ABWA)
   9820 Metcalf Avenue, Suite 110
   Overland Park, KS 66212
   (800) 228-0007
   Email: webmail@abwa.org
   Website: www.abwa.org
   Facebook: @ABWA.NationalOrganization
   Twitter: @ABWAHQ
   The ABWA provides business training and
   networking for women of diverse occupations
   and backgrounds. It hosts more than five
   thousand networking meetings each year in

more than three hundred cities across the
United States, as well as online courses
and webinars.

Canadian Small Business Women (CSBW)
6975 Meadowvale Town Center Cir 9,
Suite 320
Mississauga, ON L5N 2V7
Canada
(888) 526-9366
Website: canadiansmallbusinesswomen.ca
Facebook: @CanadianSmallBusinessWomen
Twitter: @CdnSmallBizWmn
The CSBW offers workshops, internship
opportunities, career information, and events
to help young women develop professional
skills and knowledge. Their website includes
an informational blog, a list of valuable
resources, and a directory of women-owned
small businesses.

Ellevate Network
48 West 25th Street, Sixth floor
New York, NY 10010
(646) 517-1160
Website: www.elevatenetwork.com
Facebook: @EllevateNetwork
Twitter: @EllevateNtwk

Previously known as 85 Broads, this organization empowers and connects women around the world, from the student to the professional, for networking. It offers workshops, regional chapters, and networking events.

eWomen Network
14900 Landmark Boulevard, Suite 540
Dallas, TX 75254
(972) 620-9995
Email: info@ewomennetwork.com
Website: www.ewomennetwork.com
Facebook: @ewomennetwork
Twitter: @ewomennetwork
The eWomen Network offers events, local chapters, and online tips to connect women so that they can share their skills and talents. Their mission is to help one million female entrepreneurs achieve one million dollars in annual revenue.

Office of Women's Business Ownership
US Small Business Administration
409 Third Street SW, Suite 6600
Washington, DC 20416
(202) 205-6673
Website: www.sba.gov/offices/headquarters/wbo
Facebook: @SBAgov

This office helps establish and oversee a network of women's business centers, and it provides technical assistance to women who are economically or socially disadvantaged. It also offers training and counseling, financial resources, and federal opportunities for women-owned small businesses.

Toastmasters International
23182 Arroyo Vista
Rancho Santa Margarita, CA 92688
(949) 858-8255
Email: newclubs@toastmasters.org
Website: www.toastmasters.org
Facebook: @Toastmasters International Official
    Fan Page
Twitter: @Toastmasters
Toastmasters International is an organization that is at the forefront of communication and leadership development. The organization has more than 345,000 memberships in 15,900 clubs across 142 countries. Toastmasters offers local Gavel Clubs for teens who would like to develop their leadership, public speaking, and networking skills.

Women's Enterprise Organizations of Canada
   (WEOC)
   100–207 Donald Street
   Winnipeg, MB R3C 1M5
   Canada
   (204) 988-1863
   Email: WEOCSecretariat@wecm.ca
   Website: www.weoc.ca
   Facebook: @WEOCCanada
The Women's Enterprise Organizations of
   Canada fosters networking between women
   in business, as well as offering tutoring and
   mentoring for girls. The organization focuses
   on developing the following values in business:
   integrity, professionalism, accountability,
   quality, collaboration, and innovation.

WEBSITES

Due to the changing nature of internet links, Rosen
Publishing has developed an online list of websites
related to the subject of this book. This site is updated
regularly. Please use this link to access the list:

http://www.rosenlinks.com/WITW/Network

Bernstein, Ben. *A Teen's Guide to Success: How to Be Calm, Confident, Focused.* Sanger, CA: Familius, 2013.

Bradshaw, Cheryl M. *How to Like Yourself: A Teen's Guide to Quieting Your Inner Critic and Building Lasting Self-Esteem* (The Instant Help Solutions Series). Oakland, CA: Instant Help Books, 2016.

Christen, Carol, and Richard N. Bolles. *What Color Is Your Parachute? For Teens.* Berkeley, CA: Ten Speed Press, 2015.

Clifton, Christine. *You Don't Have to Shout to Stand Out: Networking Conversations That Inspire Interest and Create Connections* (Techniques From a Quiet Entrepreneuer). New York, NY: Mindful Business Press, 2017.

Coburn, Derek. *Networking Is Not Working: Stop Collecting Business Cards and Start Making Meaningful Connections.* Washington, DC: Ideapress Publishing, 2014.

Covey, Sean. *The 7 Habits of Highly Effective Teens.* New York, NY: Touchstone, 2014.

Doyle, Shawn. *Jumpstart Your Networking: 10 Jolts to Ignite Your Networking Success.* Shippensburg, PA: Sound Wisdom, 2016.

Galley, Lauren Marie, and Kayti Welsh. *Girls Above Society—Steps to Success: An Empowerment Guide: A Teen Girl's Guide to Confidence.* Houston, Texas: Girls Above Society, 2013.

Heitkamp, Kristina Lyn. *Gay-Straight Alliances: Networking with Other Teens and Allies* (LGBTQ+ Guide to Beating Bullying). New York, NY: Rosen YA, 2017.

Lombardo, Jennifer, and Carla Mooney. *Social Networking: Staying Safe in the Online World* (Hot Topics). New York, NY: Lucent Press, 2017.

Lowe, Doug. *Networking All-in-One For Dummies.* Hoboken, NJ: For Dummies, 2016.

Macgregor, Mariam G. *Building Everyday Leadership in All Teens: Promoting Attitudes and Actions for Respect and Success.* Golden Valley, MN: Free Spirit Publishing, 2015.

Misner, Ivan, and Brian Hilliard. *Networking Like a Pro: Turning Contacts into Connections.* Irvine, CA: Entrepreneur Press, 2017

Muchnick, Justin Ross. *Teens' Guide to College & Career Planning* (Teen's Guide to College and Career Planning.) Lincoln, NE: Peterson's, 2016.

Norman, Jeff. *LinkedIn: Tell Your Story, Land the Job.* Berkeley, CA: 2015.

Perez, Nathan, and Marcia Ballinger. *The 20-Minute Networking Meeting: Learn to Network. Get a Job.* Minneapolis, MN: Career Innovations Press, 2015.

Skeen, Michelle, and Matthew McKay. *Communication Skills for Teens: How to Listen, Express, and Connect for Success.* Oakland, CA: Instant Help Books, 2016.

Thompson, Laurie Ann, and Bill Drayton. *Be a Changemaker: How to Start Something That Matters.* New York, NY: Simon Pulse/Beyond Words, 2014.

Treu, Jason. *Social Wealth: How to Build Extraordinary Relationships By Transforming the Way We Live, Love, Lead and Network.* Dallas, TX: Jason Treu Coaching, 2017.

Bolles, Richard N. *What Color Is Your Parachute?*
A Practical Manual for Job-Hunters and
Career-Changers: 2012. New York, NY:
Ten Speed Press, 2011.

Brooks, Katharine. "The Shy Job Seeker."
Psychology Today, May 23, 2010. http://www
.psychologytoday.com/blog/career
-transitions/201005/the-shy-job-seeker.

Burns, Karen. *The Amazing Adventures of Working*
Girl: Real Life Career Advice You Can Actually
Use. Philadelphia, PA: Running Press, 2008.

Casserly, Meghan. "Understanding How Women
Network." *Forbes,* October 7, 2009. http://
www.forbes.com/2009/10/07/networking
-relationships-connections-forbes-women
-entrepreneurs-men.html.

Christen, Carol, and Richard N. Bolles.
What Color Is Your Parachute? For Teens:
Discovering Yourself, Defining Your Future.
2nd ed. New York, NY: Ten Speed Press, 2010.

Dychtwald, Ken, and Daniel J. Kadlec. *The Power*
Years: A User's Guide to the Rest of Your Life.
Hoboken, NJ: Wiley, 2006.

Ferrazzi, Keith. "Networking Secret #5: Don't Be a
Networking Jerk." *Monster.com,* 2011.
http://career-advice.monster.com/job-search/
professional-networking/networking-tips
-dont-be-a-networking-jerk/article.aspx.

Garber, Janet. *I Need a Job, Now What?* New York, NY: Silver Lining Books, 2001.

Hadley, Joyce, and Betsey Sheldon. *The Smart Woman's Guide to Networking.* Franklin Lakes, NJ: Career Press, 1995.

Levinson, Jay Conrad, and David E. Perry. *Guerrilla Marketing for Job Hunters 3.0: How to Stand Out from the Crowd and Tap into the Hidden Job Market Using Social Media and 999 Other Tactics Today.* Hoboken, NJ: Wiley, 2011.

LinkedIn. "About Us." Retrieved March 24, 2017. http://press.linkedin.com/about.

Mackay, Harvey. *Dig Your Well Before You're Thirsty: The Only Networking Book You'll Ever Need.* New York, NY: Doubleday Books, 1997.

Robbins, Alexandra. *The Geeks Shall Inherit the Earth.* New York, NY: Hyperion, 2011.

Safani, Barbara. "5 Networking Lessons I Wish I Learned in High School." *The Ladders,* September 8, 2009. http://www.theladders .com/career-advice/5-networking-lessons -learned-high-school.

Singer, Thom. *Some Assembly Required: A Networking Guide for Women.* 2nd ed. Danville, CA: New Year Publishing, 2011.

Taylor, Jeff. *Monster Careers: Networking.* New York, NY: Penguin Books, 2006.

Yate, Martin. *Knock 'Em Dead Cover Letter.* 9th ed. Avon, MA: Adams Media, 2010.

Yate, Martin. *Knock 'Em Dead Resumes.* 9th ed. Avon, MA: Adams Media, 2010.

Zack, Devora. *Networking for People Who Hate Networking: A Field Guide for Introverts, the Overwhelmed, and the Underconnected.* San Francisco, CA: Berrett-Koehler, 2010.

ABOUT THE AUTHORS

Lena Koya is a scholar, teacher, and writer who lives in New York. She credits the kind and generous people with whom she has networked with building her professional career—and for developing her social circles, too!

Heather Moore Niver is a writer, editor, and poet who lives in New York State. Through her membership in the Editorial Freelancer's Association, she has used networking to connect with other local writers and editors in her area. She has participated in juried writing workshops at the New York State Writer's Institute and the Edna St. Vincent Millay Society. Every winter she leads a writing workshop at an Adirondack arts retreat.

PHOTO CREDITS

Cover VGstockstudio/Shutterstock.com; p. 7 Tanya Constantine/ Blend Images/Thinkstock; p. 11 Thomas Northcut/Photodisc/ Thinkstock; p. 13 The India Today Group/Getty Images; p. 15 Mike Moore/Getty Images; p. 19 Lucia Lambriex/Moment Mobile/ Getty Images; pp. 20–21 beer5020/iStock/Thinkstock; pp. 23, 42–43 monkeybusinessimages/iStock/Thinkstock; p. 27 Marla Aufmuth/ Getty Images; p. 32 Justin Sullivan/Getty Images; p. 33 Jamie Grill/ The Image Bank/Getty Images; p. 35 Ondine32/iStock/Thinkstock; pp. 36–37 stock-eye/iStock/Thinkstock; pp. 46–47 Jacob Ammentorp Lund/iStock/Thinkstock; pp. 48–49 fizkes/iStock/Thinkstock; pp. 54–55 HASLOO/iStock/Thinkstock; pp. 58–59 Dann Tardiff/ Corbis/Getty Images; p. 61 Rawpixel/iStock/Thinkstock; pp. 64–65 milanvirijevic/iStock/Thinkstock; p. 69 VSanandhakrishna/iStock/ Thinkstock; pp. 74–75 Tim Robberts/Taxi/Getty Images; p. 79 Bloomberg/Getty Images; p. 82 © iStockphoto.com/scyther5; p. 85 SolStock/E+/Getty Images; pp. 90–91 sturti/E+/Getty Images; p. 92 sanjeri/E+/Getty Images; cover and interior pages (globe) LuckyDesigner/Shutterstock.com; cover and interior pages background designs lulias/Shutterstock.com, Dawid Lech/ Shutterstock.com, Transia Design/Shutterstock.com.

Design & Layout: Nicole Russo-Duca; Editor & Photo Research: Elizabeth Schmermund